REVOLUTIONIZE Y

CORPORATE FAMILIES

THE NEXT EVOLUTION IN TEAMS

BRIAN DAROCHA

M·J

New York

CORPORATE FAMILIES

By Brian Darocha

© 2009 All rights reserved.

ISBN: 978-1-60037-517-0 (Paperback)

Library of Congress Control Number: 2008936940

Published by:

MORGAN · JAMES
THE ENTREPRENEURIAL PUBLISHER
www.morganjamespublishing.com

Morgan James Publishing, LLC
1225 Franklin Ave. Suite 325
Garden City, NY 11530-1693
800.485.4943
www.MorganJamesPublishing.com

Cover & Interior Designs by:

Megan Johnson
www.Johnson2Design.com
megan@Johnson2Design.com

Habitat for Humanity®
Peninsula
Building Partner

In an effort to support local communities, raise awareness and funds, Morgan James Publishing donates one percent of all book sales for the life of each book to Habitat for Humanity.

Get involved today, visit:
www.HelpHabitatForHumanity.org

ACKNOWLEDGMENTS

To my God: I humbly thank you for your grace and mercy and patience. I can think of no greater example of a loving Father than you, Lord.

To my wife, Jenny: I thank you for your love, patience, and understanding in our relationship and your brilliant help in the writing of this book. You are the love of my life, my best friend, and a wonderful mother for our children. My life is, and always will be, better with you by my side.

To my children, Sebastian, Brynna, and Elijah: Thank you for your light and laughter and constant reminder that I am always "a father in training." I will always love you.

To my family—Mom, Dad, Michael, and Sonya: Thank you for showing me what family is and how to love each other through any situation. This book would not exist without your foundation.

To my former managers, Jerry and Ramon: Thank you for the belief, support, and encouragement to "test" this concept within your organization. You are the type of leaders and visionaries that corporate America needs.

To my very first Corporate Family—Andrew, Heather, Jacqueline, Janet, Jewel, Pamela, Rosaline, and William: Thank you for your willingness to "try something new," to follow me with trust and enthusiasm, and to believe in each other. I will always think of you as family.

To the trailblazers: Team building has been around for decades. The great entrepreneurs before me have created method after method in an attempt to solve the continuing dysfunction issue. Many of these new methods are compilations of existing ones. Someone takes a piece of two or three different processes or ideas and combines them to create a "new" concept. Some processes are added to, subtracted from, or simply repackaged for a different audience. In a sense, I am doing the same thing. Time has shown us what works and what does not work. Failed teams have borne out the reality of a former concept, and we have moved on to something else in the hope that the new version will yield greater results. Were it not for those who came before me, the revolutionary idea of Corporate Families could not have been born. Knowledge combined with necessity has led me to create the Next Evolution in Teams. That knowledge was gained from some of the forerunners in team building, such as Franklin Covey and Dale Carnegie. Blair Singer, in particular, created a wonderful team building process in his book *The ABC's of Building a Business Team That Wins*. He credits "great institutions, great nations, great families and great people" for helping him develop his process, and I have incorporated several of his ideas into my Corporate Family concept. To these trailblazers and those like them, I give great thanks and all due credit.

ONTENTS

INTRODUCTION

"Team building" and "Family Values." These two terms are so overused that they lack any impact in today's world. If you asked ten people to define team building, you would get ten different definitions, although they would be fairly similar. If you asked ten people to define Family Values you would get ten very different answers. People have vague impressions of these terms and throw them around as things they need or goals they have. Managers will state that a company needs to do some "serious team building" to fix its problematic issues, but there is little thought put forth about the goals of the team building exercises and whether they will actually solve the issues in question. Politicians have a long history of declaring that they will bring the country back to traditional Family Values, but they rarely define exactly what that means to them and what impact it will have on the daily lives of Americans. These terms are not only vague but are becoming so overused that they make the speaker seem trite and unoriginal.

Knowing their history, why would I seek to combine these two overused ideas? Do two wrongs make a right? Does the lack of substance in these terms, when put together, somehow add up to a relevant idea?

Actually, I believe there is power in these terms *because* of their history. The family was the first organized institution on this planet. It has been around longer than any government, and it has survived a wide range of cultures, environments, governmental systems, and outright attacks on its very core. Family is the strongest relationship on this spinning ball of rock and water, and it has a great deal to teach us. We say that there is no bond stronger than blood. There is something deep and binding when two individuals share common DNA.

> The family was the first organized institution on this planet.

I may not speak to my distant cousins as often as I should, but the thought of someone hurting one of them makes the hair on the back of my neck stand up, my teeth clench, and a Hollywood movie script about justice and revenge begins playing in my head. It wasn't something that was outright taught by my parents, and I certainly didn't have a class on it in public school. So where did I learn such strong ideas, and how did such a strong emotional charge get ingrained in my mind regarding family? Through survival and dependency, time spent with family members, actions and intentions modeled by patriarchs, and unconditional love, I learned that family was unique in this world and worth fighting and dying for. Perhaps it is that passionate devotion that has kept families in existence and strong through the ages.

Team building, which has been around almost as long as families, has taken various forms. When two families came together to form the first tribe and worked together towards a common goal, survival, the first team was formed. When that tribe grew large, and common rules were needed, the first government was formed. The twelve tribes of Israel, the Roman Senate, the Sioux Nation, and the House of Representatives in Washington DC are all essentially teams. Some teams are more effective than others and, typically, the larger the team becomes, the more dysfunctional and ineffective it becomes. To combat this problem, we break down the big team into smaller, more manageable teams, divisions, or departments and then link them with a common goal. For example, the Sioux Nation was comprised of three large tribes: the Lakota, the Dakota, and the Nakota. Within those tribes, there were smaller, more connected units that worked together on a daily basis. The United States government has three branches: the executive, the legislative, and the judicial. The state legislatures break down the teams even further. The Department of Education, the Department of Transportation, the Department of Alcohol, Tobacco, and Firearms (ATF), and the Department of Housing and Urban Development (HUD) are all smaller units of the larger U.S. government team.

Though teams have been around for thousands of years, effectiveness continues to be a significant challenge. Different groups and individuals have struggled to work together for thousands of years. Some team building methods were not effective or mutually beneficial and caused revolts, uprisings, and revolution. Other methods were effective for the time they existed but failed in their ability to change with the culture, time, or tools. History has witnessed capitalism, communism, democracies, monarchies, theocracies, and republics. Statesmen will delight in debating the advantages and disadvantages of these ideologies and styles of government for centuries to come. The common thread in all these systems of government is the use of teams. The common thread in almost all government or business teams is dysfunction.

What if the power and security of the family could be transferred to an organization? What if Family Values (however you define them) could be instilled in a corporate environment? The compassion and deep-rooted bonds that families have are severely lacking in the corporate world. Taking a group of individuals and getting them to work as a team is a difficult task but one that is accomplished every day. Working together with the commitment of a family is another level entirely. Great sports teams become champions when their relationships evolve from a team into a family. Every corporation needs to undergo the same transformation if it wants to survive in the new millennium. Such a radical transformation can only occur one team at a time.

You are about to embark on a journey that will take your dysfunctional, unmotivated, unproductive team and transform it into an accountable, communicative, supportive Corporate Family. You are about to experience the next evolution in team building.

THE CASE FOR FAMILIES

CHAPTER ONE

STATE OF THE UNION

THE WORKFORCE AND THE WORKPLACE

BEFORE WE MOVE FORWARD OR EVEN TALK ABOUT where we are in the present, we must first look back at where we came from. How did we get here? Confucius stated it this way: "Study the past, if you would divine the future." As we travel forward, we must always evaluate where we are in relation to the past, so that we can be assured that we are on the correct path. In other words, we must look back to determine how best to move forward.

I think we all inherently know that there's a difference between our generation and our parents' generation. We also understand that our children's generation is different from ours. We tend to roll our eyes at our fathers and tell them that "it just doesn't work that way anymore," and "the times have changed." We dismiss our fathers as if their worlds are irrelevant and nonexistent. While it's true that their worlds no longer exist the way they were, those worlds are, nevertheless, part of the foundation of our current world, and the choices they have made still affect us today.

We also sadly shake our heads at our children's generation, thinking that they just don't get it. We shake our heads and complain, "They are too impulsive and lack clear direction." Some of the more outspoken of us may say, "They're sending this world to hell in a handbasket." The funny thing is that it is all about perspective. When we are kids and graduating from college in our twenties, we believe that our fathers' way is dead or dying and that we will change the world for the better. We will solve the problems they created! We think we need to throw out everything they ever did and start fresh.

When we reach the halfway mark in our professional careers (thirty to forty years old), we find ourselves disconnected from the generation we identified with in our twenties. Our viewpoints change from looking at the past with disdain, to looking at the future with disappointment. We still have the same thoughts about our fathers, but we now have a new perspective to address. Our children seem naïve and rash. We are still right. We still have the ultimate answers. But our kids seem poised to destroy the utopia we are trying to create. Our new viewpoint is one we are sure our fathers never had.

As we get closer to retirement, we notice another new viewpoint. We no longer have such strong disdain for our fathers' generation. Call it the wisdom of age; we can finally see much more clearly that our fathers had something to teach us, just as we have something to teach our successive generation, if they would only listen. How similar to our fathers we have become.

These viewpoints are critical to understand as we move forward. Most managers hire and manage people who were born at the time that they were graduating from college. Leaders from a previous generation need to know that the kids from Generation X or Y see work differently than they do. If a leader cannot meet new employees where they are, he cannot hope to lead them into the future. Just to paint a clear picture, let's look at typical recent college graduates, age twenty-two.

> If a leader cannot meet new employees where they are, he cannot hope to lead them into the future.

They were born in 1986 (where were you in 1986?).

They never owned vinyl records (perhaps have never even held one).

They never owned 8-track tapes (perhaps have never even seen one).

They may never have owned cassette tapes.

The Energizer bunny has always been going and going and going.

Rolls of film have always been processed in an hour or less.

They have always had cable TV, and it was always in color.

Charlie's Angels and Mission Impossible are movies, not TV shows.

The Tonight Show was hosted by Jay Leno. (Who was Johnny Carson?)

They weren't alive when "We Are the World" was released.

For them, there has always been only one Germany and one Vietnam.

AIDS has existed since they were born.

They were eight years old when the Internet started showing up in homes, and they have mastered every aspect of it.

They probably don't shop through catalogs and may not even shop at a lot of stores anymore.

They have always had cordless phones and cell phones.

My point is that their reality and experiences are different and that this perspective is the force shaping their expectations and desires regarding their careers. It also explains why those expectations and desires are so different from their fathers' or grandfathers' generations.

One of my former managers told me a story of his first job in the Air Force. He was in a large hangarlike room with rows and rows of five-foot metal desks. They were all facing the same direction, and they all had the same amount of space between them. It was very exact and stereotypically military. He was assigned an empty desk and told to get to work. *And he was thankful.* There weren't cubicles with six-by-six-foot L-shaped workstations. The desks weren't laid out in a "pod" configuration to enhance communication and develop a positive working environment. There weren't a lot of windows or plants. There wasn't even carpeting or adequate lighting for his desk. It was a job. And he was thankful to have it.

If a college graduate were to walk into that scene today, I am fairly certain that he would never take the job. The expectations of this new generation are drastically different from those of my former manager's generation. Some of those expectations revolve around technology and what the world can offer today as opposed to ten, twenty, thirty, or forty years ago. Some expectations are about wanting more than we had in earlier times. Whether an expectation is reasonable, justified, or acceptable, depends on what is wanted, who wants it, why they want it, and whether the company can reasonably provide it. Companies like Apple and Google have set an example by providing some of the best working environments in corporate America today. Their employees enjoy a relaxed atmosphere with so many amenities right there on the campus that the employees truly do not have to leave the compound all week if they don't want to.

> Many people today are looking for a career, not just a job.

Many people today are looking for a career, not just a job. Some are looking for a home away from home. Some are looking for security and advancement. Some are just looking for a comfortable space to collect a paycheck. You probably have people with each of these expectations working on your team. The hard part is getting the different personalities to work together. How do you get the person who views his or her job as a career and is invested in the end product to work with the person who is only there to collect a paycheck and could care less about improving and growing? The answer is a co-created set of Family Values (more about Family Values in chapter 4).

Now let's look at what workplace expectations were and how they've changed, so that we can identify what we may need to change within our own organizations in order to improve our teams.

My father started working for Western Massachusetts Electric Company (WMECo) in 1966, as a lineman climbing utility poles to fix high-voltage problems. He retired from the company in 2001. During those thirty-five years, he saw a great number of changes (the best being the creation of bucket trucks, so he didn't have to climb the poles anymore). He was a member of the International Brotherhood of Electrical Workers (IBEW Local 455) and was even the union steward for five years, navigating through a couple of strikes in the course of his tenure with the company. He went from being a lineman to being a crew chief and turned down several offers to become a salaried manager within the company. He retired from the company with a pension and full benefits, having never been fired, let go, downsized, or even transferred to another station. He was very good at his job and definitely had a talent for the work.

If I think about my father and all of the talents and gifts he has, and then think about what his passions are, I wouldn't say that he was "called" to be a lineman. It wasn't what he was "meant" to do. He remembers watching his uncle on a pole in West Virginia when he was a child and thinking that he would like to do that job someday. He saw all of the positive aspects and knew at an early age that he wanted to be a lineman. Very few people know at a young age what they want to be when they grow up. He knocked on the door of WMECo for nine months until they hired him. He wanted a career with that company. However, knowing that you want to perform a job or that you would be good at a job is different from being called to or "meant" to do a job.

My father will tell you that he enjoyed his work and that he was happy to have found that company, but also that he was "working for the weekend." In other words, he didn't seek personal fulfillment from his job. He always believed that the most he could expect from a job was a steady paycheck and security for the future. For thirty-five years, he got up at 5:30 AM and went to work. As a lineman, he was often called out after hours when there was an emergency. After, or even during, a major storm, he was outside trying to reestablish high-voltage connections. If it was a snowstorm, he was outside in −10-degree weather, trying to fix the power lines. After someone plowed a car into a utility pole that held a transformer and took out power to a whole neighborhood, he was outside in ninety-degree heat, dressed in rubber gloves, safety helmet, and heavy leather overcoat, resetting the pole and hooking up the new transformer. I am not ashamed to say that I could never do that job. Even if I had the skill and talent to do what my father did, I simply could not tolerate the conditions in which my father worked.

He has often told me of the positives about the job. He loved his crew and the other men he worked with. He loved being able to work outside in the stunning beauty of nature. After a snowstorm, he loved turning onto a country road, unaltered by a single vehicle, and seeing the sun glisten off the trees that were bent over the lane like a giant umbrella. He carried his camera with him in his truck, and he took some of the most stunning pictures I have ever seen. These positive moments are what attracted him to his job and what made his job tolerable; I would say that they were the silver lining to an otherwise dark cloud of working conditions.

Again, my father never saw his job the way I see it now, because he was looking at it with a completely different set of eyes. His expectations were not what mine are today. His reality was completely different from mine. Being a lineman for WMECo was a job. That's all it ever was. That's all he ever expected it to be. It was security for the present and for his future retirement. It was a mortgage payment, a new roof, a car repair, braces on our teeth, and shoes on our feet. It wasn't emotionally fulfilling for him, and he wasn't expecting it to be. His fulfillment came at home, in his garage, or in the yard, or in fishing on the pond behind our house or being involved with various natural preservation groups. His fulfillment came from building and remodeling our house room by room and seeing his children grow into stable, successful men and women. His fulfillment came in having a name that the entire community knew as honest, fair, and trustworthy. His job was a living.

That is how the majority of his generation viewed work. Before WWII, most of the jobs held in America were provided by local, small businesses or local/regional agricultural opportunities with a good percentage of city jobs held at manufacturing plants. When WWII started, the majority of America jumped headfirst into the war effort by working at factories, collecting raw materials, and selling war bonds. My grandfather worked at GE during and after the war. His view of work was even more stark than my father's view. His work at the factory was repetitive, mundane, and criminally unsafe by today's standards.

He and my uncle narrowly escaped death from an explosion at the plant. My uncle had just left the room, closing the fire door behind him, while my grandfather was about to put his hand on the doorknob of the door at the other end of the same room, to enter. In that moment, something went wrong, and everyone in the room was killed in an explosion.

This job was hazardous, mindless, and extremely unfulfilling ... yet he was happy to have it. My father saw the security in his work in the same way that my grandfather saw the security in his work, but my father also looked for something that he would enjoy. Ironically, my father started at the same GE plant when he moved to our town, but he knew, even as he accepted the job, that it wasn't what he wanted. You can see, in the successive generations, the desire to have more than one's father had—the expectation of more from a job than one's father expected from his. Subsequently, I want more from my job than my father wanted from his.

After WWII, corporations started growing. By the mid-eighties, corporations were starting to operate on a global scale that had not been previously seen. Today, corporate jobs are seen by many as the ultimate career opportunity. College graduates aren't looking to build a career with a local mom-and-pop store. They don't dream of retiring from the local diner, having put in a good, solid thirty-five years of waiting tables. They look for work with companies that will offer security and a future.

We must also understand that companies have changed since my father and grandfather were working and raising a family. Back in those days, the emphasis was on a skilled, blue-collar workforce. Companies were looking for people who had experience in manufacturing, manual labor, and product assembly. My grandfather wasn't concerned about getting laid off, even though he didn't have a high school diploma and had started working at age fourteen, driving a bread truck (yes, *driving* a bread truck at age fourteen). General Electric needed him because it would not have been financially feasible to train someone brand new to do his job, and there weren't a lot of extra people in the town to choose from at the time. Everyone was either already working at the factory, married to someone who was working at the factory, or was too young to work. He had some job security because of the way business operated and because of the way society was structured at that time.

When my dad was knocking on the door of WMECo with his high school diploma, he was filling a growing void. The emphasis on hiring college graduates was growing, however, and soon the requirement of a degree, technical or otherwise, would leave people like my father unemployed. At that time, companies were still looking for skilled workers, and through-out the course of my father's employ, there weren't a lot of technical graduates looking to work on utility poles. They were looking for warm and cozy inside jobs that didn't involve pull-ing high voltage in zero-degree weather. So, even though the workforce was growing and the amount of viable candidates was increasing, there was still a lack of interested workers for the job my dad was doing. During the late eighties and nine-ties, when fifty-year-old men and women were finding them-selves being downsized and watching in disbelief as their old jobs went to recent college graduates willing to work for half the money, my father still had some security.

Today, the number of college graduates is over ten times what it was in my father's day. With the emergence and acceptance of remote colleges and degrees, the number of master's degrees and PhDs has greatly increased. The volatility of the workplace due to competition, pressure for ever-increasing profits from the stock market, and the increased cost of reporting due to government regulations make layoffs a regular occurrence. The current younger generation can do many jobs from home, and they have no delusions that they will be working for the same com-pany for thirty-five years. In fact, typically,

The current younger generation can do many jobs from home, and they have no delusions that they will be working for the same company for thirty-five years.

they're looking to move and change every two to five years—whether it's their job or their company.

The company I worked for was looking for and hiring people with enough talent, skill, and potential to cover two salary bands higher than the job they were interviewing for. The company itself knew that the days when an office manager, administrative assistant, data processor, etc., stayed in the same job for ten to fifteen years, were over. In fact, if a person was in the same job for more than five years, employers started to wonder whether that employee had enough motivation and eagerness to move himself or the company forward. Such an employee began to look like an anchor, keeping the company from moving forward, just because he was someone like my father or grandfather—doing the same job for years on end. Companies are moving toward the philosophy of moving people up or out. Whether it is outright stated or inherently implied, companies and the workforce, in general, seem to understand the rules of the game. Those who don't see it are all the more confused when that reality hits them in the back of the head.

When I told my dad that I was quitting my management job in one of the best global companies around, to pursue my dream of becoming a corporate trainer/speaker, he thought I had lost my mind. In his eyes, I had made it. I had a secure job with a great company and was on the fast track to becoming a high-ranking manager earning a six-figure salary. He couldn't understand two critical points: First, there was no guarantee that, just because I did a good job, I would be able to retire with this one company. Second, it wasn't just a job to me. I wanted more out of my daily work. I wanted to do what I was called to do. I have a gift, and I want to use it to change people's lives; I felt I could do that on a grander scale if I started my own business.

My dad's point of view—the glasses that he saw work through—wouldn't allow him to see a daily job as anything other than a paycheck. For him, it wasn't about living a dream or doing what you were called to do. None of that mattered when compared to putting

His generation wasn't full of risk takers. Changing jobs, cities, or careers wasn't worth the potential when weighed against the risk.

food on the table and shoes on your children's feet. His generation wasn't full of risk takers. Changing jobs, cities, or careers wasn't worth the potential when weighed against the risk. He was a cautious man from a cautious generation, living in a time when jobs were scarce, and the next generation was more educated than the past one.

The times have changed. My generation wanted more than my father's generation. The next generation coming up wants more too. They want to know that they're using their skills and talents to the highest degree. They want to know that what they do is bettering society and/or the planet. They want more from their work environment. Rows and rows of desks are not acceptable. They want a gym, a café, and a day care, all on-site.

Some want to do their jobs from the comfort of their homes. Their expectations are as different from mine as mine were from my father's and his from my grandfather's, and we need to understand that. My grandfather wanted a job. My father wanted a job he liked. This generation wants a calling and, to a certain extent, they feel entitled to it.

As leaders, we want a communicative, accountable team that works together in a positive and proactive way. But it takes effort and insight to find out how to motivate and unite a group of people who are so drastically different. Nevertheless, if we don't understand what each team member expects from his job, his managers, and his peers, we cannot hope to succeed or even to survive in today's fast-paced business world.

CHAPTER TWO

THE FAMILY UNIT

A FAMILY IS THE PERFECT TEAM

PLAYERS, COACHES, TRAINERS, OWNERS, AND VAR-
ious other members of the sporting world have written countless books about athletic teams. They've talked about the keys
to building their teams. They've talked about the work ethic.
They've talked about common men and women with extraordi-
nary talent stepping up to the next level in order to conquer a
foe or eliminate an obstacle.

If you're an NFL fan, you have probably heard of the Green
Bay Packers in the 1960s, the Pittsburgh Steelers in the 1970s,
the San Francisco 49ers in the 1980s, the Dallas Cowboys in
the 1990s, the New England Patriots in the 2000s, and all of
the one-year championship teams in between. If you like the
NBA, you know of the legendary clashes of the Los Angeles
Lakers and the Boston Celtics, with Magic Johnson and Larry
Bird vying for the title. Even if you don't know the NBA very
well, you at least know who Michael Jordan is and what he did
for the city of Chicago and their beloved Bulls. In the MLB,

you have storied franchises like the New York Yankees, the Boston Red Sox, and the Atlanta Braves, who, throughout the recent years, have been familiar faces in the post season. For fans of the NHL, we cannot fail to mention the Montreal Canadiens, the Toronto Maple Leafs, the Vancouver Canucks, the Boston Bruins, and the Detroit Red Wings (who have dubbed their city "Hockeytown").

People have written books on just one championship year of one of these teams in one of these sports. Others have written about the dynasty of one of these teams throughout their reign and why they were able to win year after year. All of these approaches are interesting and valid and certainly have a great deal of insight to offer. However, each of these examples is interesting and newsworthy *because* it is an anomaly in the sporting world. In baseball, there are thirty teams fighting to win each year. That means there is one winner and twenty-nine losers every year. Often, the winning team holds the trophy because of luck as much as talent and skill. In 2007, the New York Yankees had a team loaded with All-Stars, Gold Glove, and Cy Young Award winners. Within the first several weeks, one of their starting pitchers fractured his leg from a line drive, their left fielder fractured his wrist on a dive for a fly ball, and several others went on the disabled list with injuries or illness.

However, there is something to be said for a team that perseveres through that type of hardship. The Yankees did make the postseason, despite their bad luck early on, and that was due in great part to the relationships within the clubhouse.

The team they had built stuck together and supported each other while the rest of the baseball world wrote them out of the postseason script.

The question, however, is this: what gets a handful of teams to the postseason and the one team to the ultimate trophy? In these types of tournaments, there is no prize for second place. As a friend of mine likes to say, "Second place is just the first loser." Why do some teams seem able to scale the seemingly insurmountable mountain to become the champions of the world? What is it about championship teams that bring them from terrible, through average, up to great, and then, ultimately, to the prize? I believe that those teams are champions because of something far deeper than a sports strategy.

> "Second place is just the first loser."

There are qualities, behaviors, and mindsets inherent in families that championship teams possess. Their coaches and leaders, either instinctively or by design, instill these traits in their teams. They know the results they want. They want a championship, and in order to get these athletes to that championship, they must get them to be a great team. Does a great team form because the coach went out to the middle of the floor or field or ice and started preaching to them about being a better team and working together? Of course not. The team bonds because the coach has created an environment that is conducive to building strong relationships. No one likes a micromanager, even in sports, and having your manager attempting to regulate your relationships like you were a marionette is the quickest path to a revolt. Some coaches and managers know how to build their teams on a fundamental level, so that their results will be at a championship level.

Miracle, a movie about the 1980 U.S. Olympic Hockey Team, was made in 2004. There is a scene in the movie that illustrates my point perfectly. This group of young, amateur athletes has been training together and playing exhibition games together for six months. For their last game before heading off to Lake Placid and the Olympics, the coach brings in a player who was at the initial tryouts. Now, instead of one player left to cut before the games, there are two, and the whole team is irritated over the idea of this new person causing an "established" teammate to lose his shot at playing. After the game, before getting on the bus, several players ask to speak to the coach. They tell him how bringing this new guy in at this late date is "crazy" and unfair. The coach explains that this kid has been playing since the tryouts, moves the puck well, has the attitude that he wants, on and off the ice, and asks why he "shouldn't be giving him a hell of a look."

"Because we're a family," they reply.

"And this is the family you want to go to Lake Placid with?" he asks.

"Definitely. Absolutely," they agree.

"This kid can help us, boys ... and I'm going to send him home."

The odds makers didn't give the U.S. team much of a shot against the established Soviets, who had won the gold every year since 1960. Most people would have attempted to stack as much talent and skill into one team as possible. In fact, that is what the United States had done in the previous winter Olympics. The U.S. All-Stars went in and got beaten over and over. The team that was going to beat the Soviets had to be talented, but they had to have something else. They couldn't just be a great team with a common goal. They had to be a family. The 1980 U.S. Olympic Hockey Team was sure of one thing: win or lose, they were going to Lake Placid and playing as a family.

What if you could learn how to instill Family Traits and Family Values in your teams, so that the result would be lower absenteeism, reduced theft, or the elimination of gossip? What if your team members became so accountable to each other that they began taking care of performance issues themselves, without your having to be a micromanager, hounding them every day of the week?

> I don't *want* a team, because teams break up. Teams lose.

All managers want a high-performing team. But corporations have been team-building for decades, and not only have the problems not been solved, but they've gotten worse. Absenteeism, gossip, lack of ownership, theft, and passing the buck, just to name a few, have all gotten worse in America's corporate teams.

I don't *want* a team, because teams break up. Teams lose. The team's best player gets lured to their most hated rival for more money. Teams are momentary. They exist for a moment in time, and then they're gone. Let's go back to the 1980 U.S. Olympic Hockey Team. What happened to them after they won? Did any of them have stellar NHL careers? Were any of them All-Stars? How many of them are in the NHL Hall of Fame? Those players, talented as they were, went their separate ways, played a little more hockey, but never re-created that magic again. When I was a manager, I wasn't interested in working really hard to obtain something that lasted a moment, only to have to create it again. I wanted to create something sustainable that produced results and got better and more cohesive as time went on. As a result, I created the Corporate Family.

The Three Essential Ingredients
That Make Families Better Than Teams

Throughout this book, and particularly in chapter 4, I talk about families and Family Traits. It is important to note that not everyone's family is the same. We all come from different backgrounds. Not everyone had a mother and a father. Some people were raised by single moms, single dads, grandparents, aunts and uncles, or foster parents. Some people lost their parents in their youth. But for the purposes of this book, I want you to think about the picturesque, stereotypical family, like in *Leave It to Beaver*, *The Waltons*, the Ingalls family in *Little House on the Prairie*, or *Father Knows Best*—the old, picture-perfect, *Pleasantville* type of images that we get. Using these images and impressions, we can achieve a neutral vantage point from

CORPORATE FAMILIES

which we can envision a Corporate Family without bringing in individual, personal baggage.

#1 Common Goal and Path

Every family must have a common goal and a path for getting to that goal. The common goal changes over time, and once it is reached, a new goal is set. The goal in a family is always just another step in the path. The parents typically set the goals, especially when the children are young. There are often several goals established at any given time, and some may be specific to individuals within the family unit.

For example, when a father or mother is laid off from a job, the family may have a goal to spend less money so that they can all survive until a new job is found. At the same time, they may be struggling to pay for some medical bills for one of the children. In an ideal family, everyone does what he or she can, to help achieve those goals. They don't complain about the lack of dinners out or the frequency of leftovers. The children save their pennies and sell lemonade or baked goods in order to contribute. Coupons are clipped for groceries, and generic food is bought in place of name brands. All of this is done so the whole family can survive, and the sick child can be treated.

You may say that it is much easier for a person to commit himself to hard work when survival is at stake. And, of course, you would be right. But what corporate team is not fighting for the survival of the company every day? In today's competitive marketplace, a complacent organization becomes an obsolete organization very quickly.

The main critical difference between a family and a team is that no individual is sacrificed in a family. No matter what the goal, no parent will "throw their child under the bus" in order to accomplish it. The well-being of the child, both physical and psychological, is paramount to a parent. In sports, there is often a motto of "sacrifice your body for the team." To win at all costs is not a rare statement. Can you picture a father telling his child to brave the ladder and clean the gutters even though it is extremely dangerous, and the child is afraid of heights? Can you hear a mother saying "suck it up, princess, and sacrifice yourself for your family"? A mother is as interested in seeing her child succeed as she is in seeing the family's goals achieved.

Corporations must invest in the continuing education and personal fulfillment of their employees if they are to increase productivity and decrease turnover. In the book *Contented Cows Give Better Milk* by Bill Catlette and Richard Hadden, the authors make the following statement: "Just as productive employees are not always satisfied, satisfied employees are not always productive." They go on to say "it's impossible for any labor-intensive business to get to (let alone stay at) the top *without* having adopted such practices." In other words, satisfied employees are not the only variable in

> Satisfied employees are not the only variable in successful companies, but those companies will find it almost impossible to be successful without satisfied employees.

successful companies, but those companies will find it almost impossible to be successful without satisfied employees.

In addition to being challenged to personal growth, an individual needs to internalize the vision and ultimate goals of the company. For example, most companies have a mission statement. If it's a large company, there may be an overall mission statement, and then each division may have a more specific mission statement that supports the company's main vision. In order to be a superior team and begin the path to becoming a Corporate Family, each team member should be able to express your mission statement in his own words, if asked. If an employee doesn't know where he's going or, more importantly, why he's going there, then he has no motivation to do anything more than the minimum required to collect his paycheck. A unifying vision gives each employee a higher cause than himself and his own selfish interests. When crafted properly, such a vision can inspire even the most divisive, un-motivated team to surprising heights of achievement.

Surveys have consistently shown that the number one reason employees are dissatisfied in their jobs has

> Everyone needs to feel like he or she is contributing to a higher purpose.

nothing to do with salary or benefits. The number one reason dissatisfied people consistently cite is that they don't feel as if their jobs have any significance or that their contributions are valued. Everyone needs to feel like he or she is contributing to a higher purpose. For a family, that purpose can be a belief system or the continued development of the family unit itself. In the case of a corporation, the higher purpose is expressed in the mission statement. You need to have employees who are invested in this higher goal.

At this point, you may be asking, how do I induce my employees to invest in the company's goals? Here are a few ideas: Post the organization's main mission statement up on a bulletin board, and put the team's individual statement on each employee's desk. Ideally, you can allow your employees to contribute to the creation of the mission statement, at least for your small team, so they can really feel a sense of ownership. Next, sit with each member of your team, and explain how the daily task he or she does affects and influences that mission statement. Show each employee how his daily tasks make a difference in the life and success of the company. Find little ways to reward your employees when their actions support the mission, and make connections to the mission whenever you give out public praise.

Almost every company has a mission statement that the employees receive from the Human Resources (HR) department when they are hired. But any employee can tell when his manager is just playing lip service to the higher goals. It is critical for you to "walk the talk": show your people that you are committed to living out these higher principles on a daily basis, and prove through your actions that you support them in doing the same.

CORPORATE FAMILIES

Every strong family has its traditions, routines, or habits. My family has holiday traditions, including setting up the Christmas tree and the outside lights on the Friday after Thanksgiving. We read two books to each child before bed and say our prayers every night. During dinner, everyone says two things that they are thankful for that day. Growing up, I can remember going to my grandmother's house to visit after bowling on Saturday mornings. We would walk in the door, get a big hug and a kiss, and have sweet tea and homemade cookies. At my Nanna's house, we would play cards or Scrabble, and she never let us win. We had to earn it. Even now, as an adult, I can vividly recall the sounds, smells, and emotions around those traditions. They hold a special place in my heart, and I know that the traditions and rituals that my wife and I are establishing now will be remembered fondly by our kids, as well. I still cherish my childhood traditions because they helped to shape the person I am today. In addition, I love to reminisce with my uncles and cousins about those moments that we shared. They are common experiences that will bind us together as a family long after my Nanna is gone.

Likewise, your team needs to have its own events or traits that distinguish it from other corporate teams, even within the same company. These rituals can be as simple as a common event or task everyone can bond around. As a manager, I instituted something called

> As a manager, I instituted something called "Three O'Clock Chocolate."

THE FAMILY UNIT

"Three O'Clock Chocolate." At three o'clock every day, I went around to every member of my Corporate Family and passed out a piece of chocolate, asking him or her how things were going that day. It allowed me an opportunity to check in with them, and it was something that the team looked forward to every day. This insignificant ritual was something special just for them. I was amazed at how protective they became of that tradition. After a while, they began to remind me if I was late or in a meeting, and three o'clock came and went without our sweet ritual. Rituals provide a sense of belonging, security, and (in the case of "Three O'Clock Chocolate") fun.

Find something that the team can do together that no other team in the company does. It has to be unique and special just to them. Maybe it's a shared song or joke every day. Maybe, every Friday, management buys bagels for breakfast. Maybe each person gets to display their favorite photos on a common board for the week so everyone can see each other's family and friends. This type of ritual strengthens the personal ties between team members and allows them to become more cohesive. You will be amazed at how team rituals increase cooperation, reduce gossip, and improve the efficiency of your team. At least one of the rituals should be daily or weekly so that ownership by every member is established quickly, and the tradition is cemented within the team.

Again, this should be something that is unique to your team, not to the building, the division, or the entire company. This is not a company-issued directive. It is a small, personal family tradition that is shared only by the members of your group. It is the uniqueness and exclusivity that give the tradition power.

#3 Family Values

There must be many rules to keep an ideal family running smoothly. Some of the rules are specific to that unit, such as "no jumping on the couch," while others are imbedded within a larger belief system, such as "honor thy father and mother." Most of the rules are tied to a larger value like "keeping children safe from physical harm" or "helping children to learn a good work ethic."

Sports teams have similar rule structures. There are rules specific to the sport that facilitate game play, rules that are set by the commission that govern all players on all teams, and rules that are set by a given team just for their players. For example, in baseball you are not allowed to physically prevent an opposing player from making a play. In other words, if a runner is rounding second, and the short stop is about to catch the fly ball, the runner can't tackle him. That rule helps to facilitate fair game play in baseball. Major League Baseball and the Players Union have agreed to rules regarding the use of steroids and the testing procedures surrounding the substance. These rules govern every player on every team in the league. On a local level, the New York Yankees manager made a rule that banned all candy and sweets from the Yankee clubhouse. Only healthy, nutritious snacks are allowed. That is a rule that only governs that team. For each of these rules, there are consequences. If the runner interferes with the catching of the ball, he is out. If a player tests positive for steroids, he can be suspended and fined. I'm not sure what the consequence is if a Yankee player is caught in the clubhouse with a chocolate bar, but I have no doubt that Joe Girardi has a swift and severe penalty in place.

In a corporation, there are also rules, accountability, and consequences. Some rules stem from a set of established ethics and are intended to enforce a minimum standard of ethical behavior. Other rules are intended to define the minimum required work hours and productivity for each employee. These rules promote fairness and provide a framework to deal with non-performers. Each corporation is different, and each has its own set of consequences. Some are as minor as a meeting, and some are as major as being fired and, possibly, sued by the company.

> As I discussed earlier, "Family Values" is a phrase that is often used but rarely defined. For our purposes, I'll define it as "rules and standards that every member of the family agrees to and believes in."

Families have their own rules and consequences. But what makes a family different is its Family Values. As I discussed earlier, "Family Values" is a phrase that is often used but rarely defined. For our purposes, I'll define it as "rules and standards that every member of the family agrees to and believes in."

In a stereotypical home, the Family Values are set by the parents and passed down to the children. The values consist of the parents' conception of acceptable ways to conduct oneself within the family unit as well as in public. These values may include rules of conduct like "don't interrupt" and "ask to be excused from the table" or rules on a higher, moral level like "do not commit adultery" and "do unto others as you would have them do unto you." These rules and morals operate on a much more personal level and are usually more specific than the general rules that govern our society.

There isn't a strict law in the United States that governs whether my children may play in our neighbor's yard. When they cross our property line and walk on the neighbors' driveway, they are not going to be arrested and charged. However, there are societal and familial rules and a code of conduct that I have taught my children, that all discourage going into a neighbor's yard without permission. In such cases, the upbringing that I have passed onto my children emphasizes politeness, respect, and asking permission.

Similarly, your team must have rules and guidelines that govern behavior not only within the team, but also during interaction with other departments. There are general rules and ethics that are set by the company, but I am suggesting the establishment of a tighter set of guidelines that are specific to your team—a set of values that are created by the team members themselves. If they participate and have input into the creation of these Family Values for your team, then every member of your Corporate Family will be completely invested in abiding by them. If you force them to agree to the rules that only you think are important, then you become a dictator. People only follow dictators out of fear.

Family Values in a corporation are not something that can be implemented through memos and official statements from the CEO. They are specific to the team and personal to every member. Establishing Family Values is critical to the success of your team. Members of your team need to know what the expectations of the group are. It doesn't matter what type of rules they come up with as long as everyone agrees to them. If there is even one person who does not agree to a value proposed, then that value must be thrown out. There is a very specific and detailed process for setting up Family Values in a corporate team, and we will go through the steps of setting up your Corporate Family in future chapters.

BUILDING YOUR
CORPORATE
FAMILIES

CHAPTER THREE

THE FOUNDATION

No SKYSCRAPER, STRIP MALL, HOUSE, OR SHED gets built without planning. Similarly, your Corporate Family is not something that you can simply throw together. Like a building contractor, you need to have a blueprint, a plan of action, and knowledge of the way your building materials interact with each other. An architectural blueprint is essential because it tells you what the house is going to look like and what materials will be used. The blueprint of your Corporate Family is just as essential.

You must know what you want your Corporate Family to look like and what functions it should perform. If you don't have in mind a clear destination for your Family, then how will you know if you get there? You must know the characteristics and traits of the members who make up the Family. If you do not know what you are creating and whom you are working with, you cannot achieve success. You cannot go to Home Depot, buy some wood, screws, drywall, and insulation, and then start building a house without a plan. You may begin to get something off the ground, but it probably won't be structurally sound, and it may even have the wrong layout for your needs.

I want you to picture building a ramshackle shed in your backyard that gets blown down in the first windstorm. What would your neighbors think of you and your efforts? Would they want your help in building their own sheds? As a manager, if you jump into building your Corporate Family without the necessary planning, and it fails miserably, do you think your boss will have faith in your skills? Do you think other companies would be interested in hiring you to come and work with their teams? Preparation and vision are critical to the success of your Corporate Family as well as your continued career. Next, we're going to look at the three parts of the foundation of your Corporate Family: the environment, the tools, and the people.

The Environment: Context and Pressure

When building a house, you need to prepare the environment. You must clear the land, grade it, and make sure it is solid enough to support your house. Of course, our Corporate Family is quite a bit different from a house built with inanimate materials. Our family members will react to our direction and change throughout the process, so we need to prepare them and ourselves for the challenge inherent in the building process.

In sporting games, there is a great deal of pressure. Depending on the sport, that pressure can last from one hour to half of a day. Games can be won and lost on one play, one error, or one moment of lost concentration. Athletes are able to bear a tremendous amount of stress. Championship teams are able to allow that pressure to bring

> In nature, everything moves to a state of more and more disorder and chaos.

them together instead of allowing it to divide them. Let's look at this from a scientific direction.

In 1977, Ilya Prigogine won the Nobel Prize in chemistry for his work on dissipative structures and their role in thermodynamic systems. His work is seen by many as a bridge between natural sciences and social sciences. In nature, everything moves to a state of more and more disorder and chaos. If a tree falls in the woods, regardless of whether or not someone hears it and whether it lies on the forest floor, it will eventually rot. It will break down and move to more and more disorder. If that same tree is buried under tons of volcanic ash, it will petrify and turn to coal. The key difference is that the buried tree is subjected to a significant amount of pressure. Pressure is a form of energy that is being applied to the tree. Without the input of energy in the form of pressure, the tree lies on the ground and rots, breaking down into simpler and more chaotic forms. The pressurized tree, however, becomes more complex and more orderly when it turns into coal. When more heat and pressure is applied, the coal turns into a diamond. Again, the material becomes more complex and stronger. Similarly, it has been proven that when a team is put under more pressure in the right environment, it will become a tighter, more cohesive unit.

Championship sports teams don't cruise through the season in a relaxed, nonpressurized environment, get to the title game, and then come together under that extreme amount of pressure. The training for the championship game begins on the first day of spring training when the players are stretching out and still getting to know each other. The coach puts them in a controlled environment and ramps up the pressure so that, when the team is in a game scenario, they won't collapse.

If you'll indulge me, I want to reference the movie *Miracle* again. There is a scene that demonstrates the effectiveness of pressure. Year after year, the Russian team beat the U.S. All-Stars. These were the best of the best from the NHL, and they lost every time. The 1980 U.S. Olympic Team was a bunch of college kids and minor leaguers that no one knew. They were put under a tremendous amount of pressure. There's a pivotal scene in the movie after the team had just played a halfhearted exhibition game against the Norwegian Nationals. The coach calls them back on the ice and makes them do drills over and over and over again. The facility turns off the lights. The assistant coach asks the coach to stop the drills. The team doctor tells him it's enough, but the coach knows they aren't a team yet. He has to push them further than they have ever gone. He has to increase the pressure. Finally, one of the players shouts out his own name, "Mike Eruzione." Then the coach asks him, "Who do you play for?" Up until this point, every player had answered that question with his college or minor league team. This time, exhausted and pushed to the very limit, it clicks, and he answers, "I play for the United States of America." The coach ends the drill. Those players were put under pressure in a controlled environment so that, when they were under pressure in a real game, they would come together instead of blowing apart and losing.

When building your Corporate Family, you must be willing to put your existing team under pressure. You must be willing to ask the hard questions and to allow uncomfortable tension to be in the room, should it arise. Nothing is solved by avoiding touchy issues or by sugarcoating the truth. You must begin your building session with an explanation that what they are about to go through may be uncomfortable at times, but is necessary to the success of the journey.

Before anything is explained, everyone must agree to take the journey together. When I began building my first Corporate Family, I didn't tell my team what we were doing beforehand. They had no idea what we were about to do so they didn't have any defenses up or preconceived notions about what a Corporate Family was. I thanked everyone for coming, and I requested full participation from everyone in the room. I assured them that they were safe to express their opinions without repercussions. I promised not to ask anyone to do anything physically impossible. Next, I requested that everyone agree to do whatever exercise I asked him or her to do and to play at 100 percent for the entire time we were there. Then, I asked them to show their agreement by raising their hands. And, finally, I asked, "Does anyone not agree to that?" It is best to ask both questions, to help avoid confusion and conflict and to underline their commitment to the agreement.

The team must also understand that this journey, while difficult and possibly emotional, is only a journey. It is a series of steps and not the final destination. There may be conflict and emotion that come up, but those moments are okay, welcomed, and temporary. There must be an agreement by everyone in the room that what is said during the building process stays in the room. What is said or what comes up for people will be resolved during the process and will not be used against them in the future. If you do not set the context that the room is safe, then you will not get honest answers and full participation and, therefore, will never fully achieve your Corporate Family.

> The environment is as important to the construction as are the other tools.

The environment is as important to the construction as are the other tools. Think of the environment as a pane of glass and the tools (the pressure, the Family Traits, the Family Values) as a beam of light. The type of glass that the light passes through will change how the light looks in the end. Is the glass clear, frosted, beveled, colored, scratched, dirty, etc? After World War I, Germany was in chaos. Out of that disaster, Adolf Hitler created a military power that was almost unstoppable. At the same time, his scientists created rocket technology and were close to finalizing the atomic bomb. But what was the environment? The hatred, oppression, fear, and violence present in the Nazi environment turned brilliant thinking into a worldwide disaster.

In contrast to Hitler's leadership is John F. Kennedy's declaration that the United States would put a man on the moon. Again, there was a great deal of pressure, but this time the environment was one of positive, unifying, and uplifting achievement. The result was that the brilliant and revolutionary ideas of the space program changed the course of human history for the better. This may seem like common sense, but you must establish a positive and safe environment if you want to build a positive, collaborative Corporate Family.

One final note about pressure: Pressure can be very uncomfortable, and as a result, many people arrange their lives to avoid it. But, as I have shown, pressure is necessary to provide the extra energy and motivation needed to transform your team. You must explain to your team that you and they have a choice. This could be a turning point in your careers. Do you want to stay in your comfort zone and slowly rot on the ground, or do you want to endure a little pressure and come together to create a diamond?

The Tools: Physical and Emotional

One of the best things about transforming your team into a Corporate Family is that it doesn't take a large budget. You don't have to take everyone on a cattle drive through Montana in order to build a cohesive unit. The physical items you'll need are a flip chart or white board, markers, paper, pens, chairs for everyone, and snacks. Depending on when you take them through the process, you may purchase lunch for the group, but that is the extent of what you will need in the room. Remember, it's not about what you buy or provide; it's about what the members of the group bring to the table on their own. They know better than you what needs to change. You just need to walk them through the process of discovering and implementing those changes.

The other key tools are honesty, participation, and acceptance. We talked about honesty and participation already. Acceptance can be tricky, depending on whom you have in your group. There needs to be an acceptance by everyone that this transformation is happening, whether they like it or not. When I took my first team through this, I stated it as bluntly as that. There may be some people who think that the functionality of the team is perfectly normal. There may be those who don't want the team to change at all. Many people fear any type of change, even that which is beneficial, because they don't want to leave their comfort zones. Some people will fear that change could put their jobs in jeopardy, and some will simply fear the possibility of extra work.

For these reasons, it is important to state at the beginning that "this team will be changing, and we will be transforming into a Corporate Family." It may appear to be a harsh and blunt statement, but it is important that there is no gray area.

You must be clear on where you stand and what your expectations are. The group must then accept the premise of that statement or else you cannot move forward. You can assure them that they will have input into the final outcome, but the transformation itself is not up for debate. After all, it is widely accepted that an organism like a team is either growing and improving or else it's stagnating and breaking down. The latter is not acceptable and, ultimately, reduces job satisfaction and security for the entire team.

Family Traits: Who Is in Your Family?

If I asked you to tell me about your personal family, you would probably have no trouble describing the personalities and character traits of your parents, brothers, sisters, cousins, etc. If you had to predict their behavior at a typical Thanksgiving, Christmas, or family reunion, you would probably be about 80 percent accurate because you know your family so well. Uncle Bob's going to drink too much, Uncle Joe will insult Aunt Cindy's cooking, Billy will break something, and Grandpa will be asleep on the couch by 2 PM. You know how they act, what their tendencies are, and how their personalities interact with each other.

Now, how well do you know your current team?

If you don't know the people on your team, you will find it almost impossible to implement true, stable change. You must know who they are, how they learn, how they interact with each other, and what their strengths and weaknesses are before

You don't hook up a thoroughbred racehorse to a farmer's wagon, and you don't put a draft horse in the Kentucky Derby

you can accomplish any type of real change. You don't hook up a thoroughbred racehorse to a farmer's wagon, and you don't put a draft horse in the Kentucky Derby. We all have different strengths, weaknesses, and talents.

But, beyond that, a manager must realize that an employee's effectiveness can often be affected by his surroundings. Many of us have experienced a time when we were superstars at our jobs. There was nothing we couldn't accomplish, and we were recognized for it. Work was fun and enjoyable, and the people we worked with seemed to be some of the best people we had ever known. Likewise, we have all experienced the opposite. Even though we were fully capable of performing the tasks listed in our job functions, we seemed to either routinely make mistakes or were miserable doing the job. We didn't like the environment we were working in or the people who were working around us. Every day was like a form of torture from which we could not escape. Are we in the right jobs, and is the environment supportive of us and our work? The answers to those questions are some of the keys to building a Corporate Family.

I interviewed a gentleman who had previously taken over managing a major call center for a large corporation. When I asked him about what he did first upon taking the position, he stated that his first step was to identify who was working for him. He put it this way: "Most of the people were in the wrong seat on the bus, and some of them shouldn't have been on the bus in the first place." He knew what many managers miss. People need to work using their strengths, talents, and passions. If there isn't a job with the company that allows them to do that, then they need to leave. They need to get off the bus, so to speak. I'm not advocating firing people for the sake of firing them, but it is not beneficial for either party to have someone in a position that he or she does not enjoy and cannot perform well. Until you identify who is on your team (who is in your family), you will continue to press blindly forward, flailing wildly at the problem while hoping and praying that it gets fixed someday. It's the shotgun method: Do a bunch of random things, and hope one of them fixes everything. Throw something out there, and hope it sticks. I prefer the "do it once, do it right" method.

We are used to hearing that there are three main ways that people learn: visual, auditory, and kinesthetic. Dr. Howard Gardner wrote two books, *Frames of Mind: The Theory of Multiple Intelligences and Intelligence Reframed*, in which he explained his Multiple Intelligence Theory and the nine intelligences that people possess. I recommend reading these two books to get the full explanation of his findings, as I will not do them justice. (Were I "King of the World," I would make these two books required reading for all teachers and instructors, no matter the grade level they're teaching.) I will give brief descriptions of these nine intelligences and then align them with familial archetypes, so that you can more easily identify whom you have in your Corporate Family. Every person is born with all nine of these intelligences but is usually dominant in one, sometimes two, specific ones.

Intelligence #1: Verbal Linguistic (Word Smart)

This intelligence refers to the ability of the person to manipulate words and language, both spoken and written. Howard Gardner wrote in *Frames of Mind* that a person strong in this intelligence has the following traits:

> A sensitivity to the order among words—the capacity to follow rules of grammar, and, on carefully selected occasions, to violate them. At a somewhat more sensory level—a sensitivity to the sounds, rhythms, inflections, and meters of words—that ability which can make even poetry in a foreign tongue beautiful to hear. And a sensitivity to the different functions of language—its potential to excite, convince, stimulate, convey information, or simply to please.

Essentially, they are good storytellers, able to easily use words to evoke emotion and craft arguments. Gardner also wrote that T. S. Eliot believed "the logic of the poet is as severe, though differently placed, as the logic of a scientist." Professions that rely heavily on this intelligence are attorneys, writers, speakers, and politicians. Dr. Martin Luther King, Jr., John F. Kennedy, and Ernest Hemingway are a few individuals who were gifted in this area.

Intelligence #2: Logical/Mathematical (Math Smart)

This intelligence refers to the ability of a person to work with numbers and data. Our great scientists, engineers, and researchers have a high aptitude in this area. They naturally see patterns, groups, and trends and are more comfortable working with the true/false and right/wrong of numbers as well as on complex logic puzzles and statements. Two statements in Gardner's book effectively define this intelligence:

> "It seems evident that mathematical talent requires the ability to discover a promising idea and then to draw out its implications."

> "At the center of mathematical prowess lies the ability to recognize significant problems and then to solve them."

Albert Einstein and the NASA scientists who put a man on the moon are obvious examples of people who have exceptional abilities in this type of intelligence.

Intelligence #3: Visual/Spatial (Art Smart)

This person has the ability to form and manipulate objects spatially. He can often look at a room and know if the furniture is going to fit. He can look at an object and see it from every angle. He can mentally twist and turn it to determine if it will fit through a door, connect with another object, etc. He learns the most from visual presentations like movies, pictures, PowerPoint presentations, graphs, and flip charts. If he can see it, then he will understand it. He is good with maps and would never deign to ask for directions. Interior designers, artists, sculptors, and craftsmen are high in this intelligence. People like Pablo Picasso, Leonardo da Vinci, and Bobby Fischer are examples.

Intelligence #4: Bodily/Kinesthetic (Body Smart)

As you would expect, in this type of intelligence, input is gathered through the body. Gardner states it this way: "Characteristic of such an intelligence is the ability to use one's body in highly differentiated and skilled ways, for expressive as well as goal-directed purposes." People high in this intelligence are physical and coordinated. Our great athletes, Olympians, dancers, and martial artists are exceptional in this area. Through physical interaction and repetition, these individuals learn and develop. Marcel Marceau, Michael Jordan, Jackie Chan, and Mikhail Baryshnikov embody this intelligence.

Intelligence #5: Musical (Music Smart)

This intelligence is in tune with the rhythms, tones, and melodies of the world around us. A person who is outstanding in this area has the ability to think in, understand, and create music and rhythm. She usually has a beat in her head and enjoys learning through rhythm and rhymes such as "Columbus sailed the ocean blue in fourteen hundred and ninety-two." Wolfgang Amadeus Mozart and Louis Armstrong are obvious examples, but I would say that Dr. Seuss was strong in this as well; even though he falls heavily in the "word smart" category, the rhythm and melody that his words created display a significant aptitude in musical intelligence as well.

Intelligence #6: Interpersonal (People Smart)

This person has the ability to interpret and respond to the moods and emotions of other people. He is sensitive and empathetic and is in touch with his emotions. He genuinely cares about people and invests himself in the lives of others. Gandhi, Oprah, and Bill Clinton are good examples of this intelligence.

Intelligence #7: Intrapersonal (Self Smart)

The ability to know one's self, although rare in our fast-paced society, is necessary before true personal growth can occur. A person with intrapersonal intelligence knows his strengths and weaknesses, where he stands on issues, and what motivates him. Usually time and reflection are required in order for someone to develop this intelligence, but there are some who are naturally gifted. Those who are pursuing careers in psychology and sociology are often well versed in the intra- and interpersonal intelligences. Also, writers and poets are often very strong in this intelligence. For example, Maya Angelou writes from a place of great self-awareness.

Intelligence #8: Naturalistic (Nature Smart)

A person high in this intelligence is highly aware of her environment. She notices the different materials in the world around her and how they progress and interact (grass to marble to metal to glass). He has a strong sense of categorizing. He may have a passion for studying the different types of plants and animals and feel the most calm and productive when in an environment where he can hear birds, feel the wind, and breathe fresh air. Charles Darwin is an example of this intelligence.

Intelligence #9: Existential (Spirit or Life Smart)

Whether or not this is a true innate intelligence—or just the product of life experience—can be debated. Gardner defines it as the ability to pose and ponder questions regarding life and death. He says it is the ability to ask the tough questions and then think through the possible answers and repercussions regarding those questions. The great philosophers and religious leaders of our time are strong in this intelligence. Plato, Socrates, and C. S. Lewis are examples of this.

NOW THAT YOU HAVE A GLIMPSE OF HOW PEOPLE learn and the different intelligences they may be gifted in, you can apply this knowledge to the team members in your new Corporate Family. We all understand that there are as many personality traits and skill set combinations as there are people on this planet. Each person is unique and has within himself specific experiences and talents that have shaped him from childhood. No book or study could possibly cover all the possibilities. Instead, I have categorized the stereotypical personalities and matched each one with an icon of a typical family member. It is my hope that the icons will remind you of someone in your own family or organization and will help make these concepts easier to remember and work with. As we move forward, we will be talking about the characteristics of these family member icons, what they bring to the table, and how they may interact.

At this point, I must pause to reiterate that not everyone will have a family similar to the type of family I am describing here. I understand that we all come from different backgrounds. Maybe you didn't have a mom or you hated your dad. Maybe you don't have any brothers or sisters. Or maybe you never knew your uncles, cousins, grandfathers, or grandmothers. When I talk about these stereotypes, what I am talking about are the personalities and the skills and the gifts these people bring to the typical family unit. Please try not to get caught up in the fact that you may not know anyone who exactly fits the stereotypical roles I outline here. The purpose of discussing these roles is to give you some simple images you can use to help you understand and define the traits you observe in your team members. Everyone in our individual families—every single member—has strengths and weaknesses. But they all bring something positive to the family unit. They all contribute in some way. Your job is to recognize those positive strengths and determine how best to use them in forming an effective Corporate Family.

As we move forward, bring back to mind the shows and pictures I mentioned before: *Leave It to Beaver*, *The Waltons*, and *Little House on the Prairie*. They are clichés and may seem unrealistic and out-of-date, but they are tools to get you to think abstractly about the terms "Mom" and "Dad" without bringing in any personal baggage or individual issues surrounding those words. If you find yourself thinking "that wasn't what my dad was like" or "my mom couldn't do those sorts of things," then I ask that you refer back to one of the examples that I just provided, so that you can get the nugget of what I'm saying without letting any personal issues derail you.

The first role I would like to describe is the Mom because she is one of my favorites. The Mom is the nurturer. She is someone who cares about what is going on within the family and is tuned in to the group dynamic. The Mom intuitively knows when someone is having a bad day, and she is, in many respects, the thermometer of the family. Imagine that she walks around taking the temperatures of her family or team members, to see where they are emotionally in a given moment. It's almost like she has a sixth sense about people. She *knows* when somebody is upset or when two people don't get along.

In the corporate world, she knows what is going on personally with everyone on her team. Who is having a birthday? Who is expecting a baby or having trouble conceiving? Whose son is graduating from high school? Whose daughter is in a ballet recital this week? Who is having personal issues that may be interfering with work? The Mom type knows all these things because she is invested in her family. She is like the glue that holds the different personalities together.

One of the Mom's greatest gifts is organization. My mom was a genius at organizing, and I have found that most women are uncanny multitaskers. If a man says that he is a great multitasker, then you can be sure that one of two things is true: either he is an anomaly in this world, or he is lying through his teeth. Guys tend to be task-oriented. When I worked in a corporate office, I found that I had to focus on one thing, finish it, and then go on to the next thing. But because women are typically multitaskers, their focus can be on three different things at once. This tendency is also the reason why my wife has no trouble holding a serious conversation while also keeping track of the sitcom playing on our TV, but I never hear a word she says at these times.

My mom is a great example of multitasking as well. I remember being in the kitchen watching my mom cook dinner. But my mom didn't just cook dinner; she was the ringmaster of Barnum and Bailey's worldwide traveling three-ring kitchen circus. She was amazing. Let me paint you a picture of a typical night from my childhood: She's standing in the kitchen, cooking multiple things at once—broccoli, spaghetti, and sauce on the stove and bread in the oven. At the same time that she is cooking dinner, she is on the phone. Now, this is back before we had cordless phones, so she is talking on a phone with a fifteen-foot, curly cord stretching across the whole kitchen. During her conversation, she is also washing dirty dishes (apparently she didn't have enough to occupy her time). On top of this, she also has three kids in various stages of disarray. I, being the youngest, am probably the most annoying in the scenario because I am asking her questions and generally being underfoot. My sister is showing my mom her homework and asking for approval. My brother just wants to know if he can keep working on repairing his bike—or is dinner almost ready? While all of this is happening, my mom is continuing to wrap herself up in and then untangle herself from and step over and dance with this phone cord like she's on *Dancing with the Stars*. Somehow, through all of this, the questions get answered, the

CORPORATE FAMILIES

homework gets approved, the children feel acknowledged, the dishes get done, the food finishes *at the same time* (and it's delicious), and the person she's been talking to on the phone feels like he or she has had a complete, attentive conversation. This is the type of skill that the Mom brings to the family. She is the ultimate multitasker. She holds the entire unit together.

In terms of intelligences, the Mom is very strong in the interpersonal area. She may have some intrapersonal awareness but is often more in tune with others than with herself. She is usually sacrificial with her time and workload if it means helping someone in need. Due to the organized nature of Mom, she has some naturalistic intelligence as well, but most of her strength and power lies in the interpersonal area.

Dad

Dad is typically the disciplinarian in the family. The phrase "wait till your father gets home" is etched into the American psyche. He is the leader of the household and typically has the final say in matters (although he is heavily influenced by Mom). Dads see in absolutes. The situation is black or white, right or wrong, yes or no. There is very little gray area for the Dads, and they don't like for a decision to be questioned. Because of this inflexible personality, Dads can be short-tempered and can get frustrated very easily. I often say that Dads have a short fuse with a very loud bang, and you don't want to light the fuse. Ironically, every family member knows how to light the fuse and push the buttons on Dad in just the right way to set him off. Many children, as they get older, learn to bring Dad close to the point of explosion and then defuse the bomb with two seconds left on the timer. Children learn very quickly how to manipulate their parents. When my daughter turned two, I realized that she had me figured out, trained, and wrapped around her finger without my knowing it until that time.

A Dad is also the "go-to" guy in the house. If something needs to be fixed, you bring it to Dad. If something needs to be obtained at the last minute, then you can count on Dad. If there is a science project that needs to be turned in tomorrow, then Dad will figure out how to get it done. He can always be counted on, when the chips are down, to come through in the clutch. The family naturally looks to Dad for answers, solutions, and solidity. Because he sees in absolutes, he is often relied upon when the world seems to be getting out of control. When the family is stretched thin and involved in more groups, sports, and projects than they can handle, they look to Dad to restore order by making some hard choices or by leading the charge to success.

Dads are task-oriented and rather compartmentalized. There is a book modeled after the Mars/Venus concept called *Men Are Like Waffles, Women Are Like Spaghetti* by Bill Farrel and Pam Farrel. It's a great analogy, and it essentially states that each man lives like a waffle—one square at a time. They are in one square, they focus on that square, and when they are done with that square, they move on to the next square. Nothing in the former square affects the square they are in now, and nothing in this square will affect the square they go to next. It is very compartmentalized. Women, on the other hand, are like spaghetti. Everything touches everything else. Everything is intertwined. Everything is relationship-oriented. Everything is fluid and affects everything else. Men, living in their waffles, can turn one square on and the other off, and never the twain shall meet. "I understand you're mad at me for that, but now that we're talking about this new subject, you shouldn't be mad at me anymore." That type of thought process makes perfect sense to a man. Everything is step by step—one, then two, then three. Dad is a very logical creature.

Because of this logical makeup and the way Dads lead the charge with quick solutions, they are often seen as natural managers and leaders. There are a large number of Dad stereotypes who are in management positions for the simple reason that they can make decisions. Right or wrong, they have stepped up and made a decision on a project or issue that has allowed the company or team to get out of the stagnant place it was in and move forward toward productivity. I have known many managers who were identified early in their careers as having leadership potential, mainly because they were making decisions outside their pay scale. They chose to "do" instead of "ask," and, therefore, they were looked upon as individuals who had vision and

Dads are action takers and prefer not to deliberate for hours on end.

courage, not people who overstepped their bounds. Dads are action takers and prefer not to deliberate for hours on end. They want the data quickly and then want to move forward with a decision right away.

In the area of multiple intelligences, Dads are often strongest in visual intelligence. They are comfortable in the space of a room, whether it is a conference room with a handful of people or a large meeting of fifty to a hundred people or more. They see and work well with flip charts, organizational charts, pictures, graphs, etc. Because we live in a highly visual world, someone who is naturally adept in this intelligence makes for a logical choice for management when a promotional opportunity presents itself. He will think, write, speak, and present in a visual way, so that those who are also strong in this area, typically other managers higher up the ladder who are interviewing him for a leadership position, find they have a connection with this candidate, visualize him in the role, and see him as the logical hiring choice. Because it is human nature to be attracted to those like us and to naturally group ourselves with those we have things in common with, it is obvious why a spatial person would lean toward hiring another spatial person instinctively. In other words, without rules or guidelines, ruled only by "gut instinct," people will tend to hire and promote those like themselves.

That is why understanding these multiple intelligences—who has them and which ones you need in your Corporate Family—is so important. If you were putting together a team for a project and only brought in people who were like you, then you would not achieve a well-rounded solution because you would have excluded anyone who might be able to see the other sides of the issue.

Sister

Sister has some similarities to Mom, but is different in several areas. Sister is relationship-oriented, but she is more gossipy and more of a busybody. She knows what is going on with everyone, like Mom, but talks about it without permission. Sister is also current on all the information within the company and on the relationships between teams and individuals. She has a knack for knowing what is going to happen before it actually transpires, and she prides herself on being the first one to know something. In the corporate world, upper management tends to hold information close until they are ready to make an official announcement. If Sister somehow knows some of the given information but not the whole picture, then she will inevitably fill in the blanks on her own. This speculation causes great stress to her fellow employees and upper management, who must now deal with the rumors and gossip that are destroying the company's morale.

> If Sister somehow knows some of the given information but not the whole picture, then she will inevitably fill in the blanks on her own.

Before I left my last job, the company was looking at the possibility of consolidating the different customer service groups into one entity, under one management structure, and moving them into one building. What "Sister" found out was that we were consolidating, and she mistakenly assumed that jobs would be eliminated. The rumor mill got hold of that idea and ran with it until it had been blown completely out of proportion. After several days of stress and gossip, we were able to assure everyone that the elimination of jobs was not even a remote possibility. Had "Sister" not gotten ahold of a piece of information and filled in the blanks as she had, then the rest of her teammates would not have gone through the stressful prospect of downsizing.

Sister is trendy and up on all that is popular but can be very emotional as well. Sister is also very, very fast at getting jobs done; however, accuracy is often sacrificed for speed. You can get it done fast, but it won't be necessarily right. She is less of a multitasker than Mom, so she can be considered a cross between Mom and Dad, in that respect (which makes sense, given that she is their offspring). She is sporadic and mercurial, but if you need something done quickly, and you can eliminate outside distractions that may cause sloppiness, then she is the one who can get it done for you. If the job or conversation is something that she is interested in, then her ability to focus on it and complete it quickly is unparalleled. However, if she gets bored with the job or distracted by something more interesting, then she will find ways to justify switching to another job or task and not completing the original assignment.

As I stated, Sister has some similarities to Mom. They both share the interpersonal intelligence, although Sister does not have the awareness of how her actions affect others around her. She is interested in what is going on with others although not for any genuine interest in their lives, but more because information is fun to gain and pass on. Sister does not have the intrapersonal intelligence as Mom does, but she is strong in the musical intelligence area. I am not suggesting that all Sister personalities will show an ability to create or compose music. Rather, I am alluding to the fact that Sister always seems to have a rhythm to her. She lives her life in concert with a beat and melody that are constantly running. Conversations with her tend to have a distinct pace and beat to them, and she seems to always have a song in her head. Often, her speech patterns will have a tempo and, at times, a melodic flow to them—almost as if she were singing the words. If you can match her tempo with a job or a job with her tempo, then she can be a great driving force toward accomplishing your goals for the day, week, month, quarter, or year.

Brother

As is typical in many families, Brother is 180 degrees opposite from Sister. The Brother stereotype is the loner of the group and doesn't interact much with others unless forcibly placed in a social situation. It is not that he suffers from enochlophobia (fear of crowds) or agoraphobia (fear of open spaces or of being in crowded, public places); it is just that he prefers to work alone and to work with things rather than with people. Simply stated, he is an introvert and not an extrovert. He is analytical and is content to observe a situation or discussion rather than contribute to it. He will voice his opinion if asked but rarely gives it freely. He prefers direct questions that speak to the issue at hand and have a quantifiable answer. If your question falls directly into his realm of expertise, then be prepared for a lengthy and detailed answer. The old adage of "ask him the time, and he'll tell you how to build a watch" fits brother to a T. Many engineers working today are Brother stereotypes.

> Brother is not political and prefers the direct, blunt answer, as it is the truth, and the truth does not need to be softened or sugarcoated.

Brother is not political and prefers the direct, blunt answer, as it is the truth, and the truth does not need to be softened or sugarcoated. This style of interaction often gets him in trouble because many people interpret how a message is delivered, in addition to what the message contains. Brother often winds up insulting, dismissing, or generally upsetting those he's talking to, without realizing it. It is important to understand that he is not being intentionally hurtful or malicious with his comments and explanations. He is merely delivering the facts of the situation. Because of his concrete way of thinking and because his answers are rooted in data, math, and analytical thinking, he tends to find other options difficult to entertain.

When there are two choices, and one is rooted in data and logic while the other is based on personalities and morale, he can really only see the choice based on logic. Brother will tend to dig his heels in and argue his point with the sole objective being to convince you why this is the right way to do something or why this is the right course of action. He believes that the reason you aren't agreeing with him is because you don't understand the information. Even when you try to exit the discussion, he will continue to argue. Again, it isn't out of malice but out of a logical frame of mind, intent on convincing you why he is right. This is the course of action that gets him in the most social trouble and is also why others find him difficult to work with.

There is a great deal of loyalty at the core of Brother, and he will stay with a company longer than most people, mainly due to his way of seeing everything as an equation. "I have given this much, and the company has given me this much back. Therefore, I should remain loyal." This is usually communicated with the following phrase: "They've been good to me and my family." As long as Brother is continually challenged and not taken for granted, he will be a good and loyal asset to the business for a long time.

As you probably guessed, Brother is the poster child for the logical/mathematical intelligence. He is data-driven and seeks to obtain the right answer for the problem at hand. Obviously, there are roles and jobs that Brother is perfect for and others that he should stay away from. Direct, front-end contact with your customers is probably not the best situation for Brother, whereas research and development is much more in line with his talents, gifts, and personality. There are also projects that will need Brother at certain stages. Perhaps you are seeking to create a new product for your company. Brother is essential during the brainstorming, designing, and testing stages. After those steps are completed and you begin to move toward marketing and sales, Brother won't have a lot of input to give, as you are now dealing with how the product is perceived by the buying public who typically purchase based on emotion and not on logic. Not every team needs a Brother on it, and those that do probably don't need him for the duration of the project—but when his expertise is needed, he is essential to its success.

Brother is also strong in the naturalistic intelligence area, as it deals with categorizing and studying relationships and patterns within data. While Brother may not be happy roaming around the woods, learning which mushrooms are deadly and which are edible, he is at ease comparing and sorting the data available and, therefore, has aptitude in naturalistic intelligence.

Grandparent

It doesn't matter whether you choose to think of this stereotype as a grandmother or a grandfather because we're not talking about gender. We are merely attempting to identify the different skills and traits that team members have and associate them with family member archetypes.

The Grandparent is the person who knows it all, has seen it all, and, most importantly, remembers it all. What was it like during World War II? Just ask Grandpa. What was it like before the microwave oven? Go and ask Grandma. The Grandparent is your link to the past—the keeper of knowledge not detailed in history books. He or she is very calm and very patient. He listens, he analyzes, and then he gives you the answer you need, but, unlike Brother's, his answers come from experience and not from data. He will give you the right answer almost every time, because he has seen it all. Grandparent has probably seen the right answer, then watched as it was later eliminated, and then witnessed it come back around again.

I had a field engineer in Louisiana whom I enjoyed talking to as long as I had the time. He had a thick Southern drawl, an eternally positive attitude, and a general easy way about him. I remember communicating to him a recent change in procedure. He gave me a chuckle and said, "Mr. Brian (pronounced 'Brine'), that's the way we were doin' it five years ago. I'll tell you what ... I'll just keep doin' it my way, and five years from now, we'll match up again."

Sometimes, in a company that has been around for a long time, you will find that the decisions that Dad is making are the same ones that were made ten years ago. The Grandparent knows why it did or did not work then, why it was abandoned, and why it will or will not work now.

The Grandparent's experience, everything that he has done and gone through, will not be found in any manual or Standard Operating Procedure.

The knowledge and history that he possesses is essential. It is very difficult to lose a Grandparent, because what he knows, he doesn't often pass down to the next generation. It is very difficult to capture that knowledge in a shared medium. The Grandparent's experience, everything that he has done and gone through, will not be found in any manual or Standard Operating Procedure. The Grandparents are the ones who can look at a situation and intuitively feel what is going on, what the right path is, and how to go about implementing that path.

One of the major flaws with Grandparents, however, is that they are extraordinarily slow. They work at their own pace, and that pace is usually tortoise speed. In the everyday world, the typical grandparent is doing forty miles per hour in a fifty-five zone. In the corporate world, when millions of dollars can be lost every minute, you find yourself begging the Grandparent, "Could you just get me an answer, please? Just tell me what I need to know, so I can move on to the next thing." In this fast-paced world, it is mind-boggling how anyone can move at such a slow pace. Some of the inexperienced employees will wonder why the company hasn't fired these roadblocks to efficiency, but the experienced, veteran managers know what an asset they are. Managers desperately need that knowledge base and the Grandparent's years of experience, to help to avoid repeating bad history and future, unseen potholes. The Grandparent is an essential member of every corporation, family, and Corporate Family.

Grandparents use multiple types of intelligence, sharing aspects with other members of the family. They have good interpersonal and intrapersonal awareness, like Mom, but they also possess one that no other family member has: existential intelligence. Whether it is inherent to their core, genetic from birth, or simply a product of the wisdom of age, Grandparents have not only the ability to see issues from a larger, higher perspective, but the patience to wait for the forthcoming answer as well. Often they are searching through their minds for wisdom, not just a quick answer; however, this time-consuming searching can often be aggravating to others. When I would ask my mentor for advice, he would often clarify with this statement: "You can ask me for my *opinion*, which I can give you right now, and you can do whatever you want with it. Or, you can ask me for my *advice*, which may take several days for me to give, and I expect you to follow it." He had great wisdom and often asked questions that were so deep that I discovered new levels within the question and the answer, years after the question was originally asked. Higher knowledge, perhaps originating from knowing oneself so well, as well as from a lifetime of interacting with others, is so rare in this fast-paced, instant-gratification world, that a Grandparent on your team and in your family is to be cherished. Through their existential intelligence, they will often act as the ethical and moral litmus paper test for a team, project, or company.

Cousin

The last family member that we will discuss is the Cousin. The Cousin has some great positives to bring but also some negatives as well. I will have to break up the description of the

Cousin into two parts, as there are two different versions of him. The first version is genuine, and the second is a mask. We'll start with the genuine personality.

The genuine Cousin has an outgoing, personable character. He is known to be a good storyteller, funny, athletic, and knowledgeable about a lot of subjects. He often watches the news and sport highlights, so that he won't be caught off guard or be unaware of what is happening in the world. He always seems to be extremely optimistic, and believes that anytime something starts to go wrong, it will all somehow come out right.

In the corporate world, the Cousin brings some interesting things to the table. He is the jokester, the one who brings levity to the group, and that is very important in stressful times. When the group dynamic starts getting a little off-balance, or you're getting close to a deadline, or there's high pressure, it is the Cousin who breaks the tension. One of his best tools is randomness—something that catches you completely by surprise. He's the type of guy who will come back from lunch with ice cream sandwiches for everyone, just as a tension breaker or to get a smile and make someone's day. He is very genuine and revels in others thinking of him as weird, strange, odd, and unpredictable (but in a good way). The stories and jokes he tells will have you laughing and rolling on the floor in no time.

Cousin actually reminds me a lot of my brother and me. I am the youngest of three, so by the time I got married and had a family, my brother and sister had already been married for several years, and each had two children of their own. So, when my kids were born, my brother turned into the crazy uncle, and it was great to watch. As an example, when my brother comes to visit me, within five minutes of walking through my door, he adopts a voice other than his normal one, usually sounding like some animated character from a movie or cartoon show, and it will have the intended effect on my children: unstoppable belly laughs. I have to admit that I am right there with him in this game. To my nieces and nephew, I'm Crazy Uncle Brian.

I should have known that the two of us would end up like this, given our behavior when we were kids. We did strange and amusing voices all of the time. One night, we had our parents laughing so hard while they were driving down the road that we almost ended up crashing several times. He and I were in the backseat reciting word for word, voices and all, *What's Opera, Doc?*, the old Bugs Bunny cartoon. He was doing the Elmer Fudd part, and I was doing Bugs Bunny, and we sang the entire thing. My parents were laughing so hard that they had tears rolling down their faces, and their eyes were practically clamped shut. I distinctly remember three close calls with the guardrails before we made it safely home. That wasn't unusual for us. That was just the kind of family we were, and our kind of personalities are a large part of Cousin's role.

The Cousin keeps things light and helps to relieve tension, and that is a much-needed role on the team. If you can't have fun and enjoy what you do, then you will not stay in your job for very long. Either you'll get fed up and quit, your attitude toward your job will be noticed, and you'll be fired, or you will subconsciously sabotage your work, forcing your manager to fire you, or you'll die from stress and unhappiness, having given your soul and joy to a job you hate in exchange for a paycheck. Cousin helps bring some joy and fun into the workspace, so that those who are having a difficult day or are overwhelmed by a large project will have the relief they so desperately need.

One of Cousin's issues is that, due to all of this random levity, there are times when he doesn't get as much work done as he could. If this line is crossed, it can affect how he is perceived by his team/family. People will appreciate the levity and humor but not at the expense of the work—and not if it creates more work for them. "He's a funny guy" can turn quickly into "I wish he would stop with the jokes and actually do some work." It's a balancing act, a fine line that must be walked carefully.

The second version of Cousin is the disingenuous one— the one who wears a mask and merely puts forth the persona of what I have described. Cousins, both versions, are good at public relations and are great salesmen. Those they interact with typically love them, enjoy being around them, and speak highly of them to others. This second version, however, is simply playing a good game, putting on a good show, and wearing a good mask, and people are often taken in by that persona. However, those within his family who know him best usually have an opinion that is 180 degrees opposite.

Those who know him will often state that the Cousin is abrasive, blunt, demanding, and arrogant. Cousin will often tell you what he thinks of you, whether you want to hear it or not. This version watches the news and sports, just so he can sound smart and have topics of conversation to use to schmooze clients. Everything that the public sees is a mask and a falsehood—they will never discover the Cousin's real personality.

Whether the Cousin is a direct employee or an authorized representative working in a contractor status for the company makes no difference, as he is representing the corporation and its products to the general public. Let me be clear: Cousins are essential to an organization, but which version you employ is paramount to your company's long-term success. I would encourage everyone to act on an ethical level and employ only those who are genuine and truthful—avoid the second version of Cousin, if possible. The second version may make the company more money as a salesman in the short term, but the negative effect that this employee can have on your support personnel and overall reputation can be severe.

> Cousins are essential to an organization, but which version you employ is paramount to your company's long-term success.

Cousin has talents in three of the multiple intelligences: verbal, kinesthetic, and interpersonal. His humor and levity are rooted in both verbal and physical comedy. Whether he's telling jokes, doing impersonations, or performing the "Running Man" dance out the door at 5 PM, he is using these intelligences. People are naturally attracted to him because of his strong verbal communication skills, but he also seems comfortable with his body. He uses his body and facial expressions to enhance stories and communicate effectively, especially in a salesman's role. Aptitude in the kinesthetic intelligence area also allows him to have a cursory ability in sports. He may not be at a professional level in his ability, but he can hold his own and not embarrass himself on the golf course, tennis court, or softball field.

His interpersonal skills are more rooted in the back-and-forth communication and problem solving between him and his clients or team/family members. The genuine Cousin is honestly interested in solving problems and making people laugh through his humor and levity. The disingenuous Cousin is only interested in providing solutions that will make him and his company wealthy. Both may exhibit the same behavior, but when the objective is solely monetary, the other person involved in the discussion or transaction will often be aware of it and be unhappy with the purchase, even though it may be exactly what he needed. Any negative thought regarding the product, communication, service, or company will prevent that person from becoming a repeat customer. Which version of Cousin you have selling for you will determine the mindset of your client and will therefore determine if that client will continue his relationship with your company.

The Family

We now have a family: Mom and Dad, Brother and Sister, the Grandparent, and the Cousin. This is your family, and there are reasons why you have this family. There are reasons why every member of your family is present at any given point. Despite all their flaws, you need every member of your family, or at least some aspects of your family, at some point. From Brother's analytical analysis to Dad's decision making, to Mom's ability to ground the family during the implementation processes, to Sister's perspective on the external perception of the decision, to the Grandparent's expertise and history, to the Cousin's salesmanship—you will need everyone. There are pros and cons to all of the family members. There are things that are great about them and things that are difficult. Working through those differences is a balancing act that is easier when you know who you have on your team, what their main learning and communication styles are and how they may interact.

When you inherit a family, it's important to discover who is in that family very quickly. Those of you who have gotten married know that you have to figure out the in-laws. How much of the Mom personality is in your new mom and how much of the Dad personality is in your new dad? How much of Brother or Cousin is in your new dad, and how much of the Grandparent is in your new mom? These are the kinds of things you have to figure out with your real family as well as your Corporate Family.

When you have the opportunity to build your own family from scratch, knowing who you need is essential. If you don't

> You need to be looking for a good combination of personalities, not just the next person through the door.

know, then you can't possibly work through the personality issues. You won't have a clear grasp of how they are interacting. You won't know whom you are missing and therefore whom to look for when you're going through a hiring phase. You need to be looking for a good combination of personalities, not just the next person through the door. What are the objectives of the company, division, or separate project, and who is best suited to accomplish those goals? Once you know that, you can hire or appoint the personalities and skill sets you need in order to accomplish those goals. The amount of time and energy that you will save by having the right people in the right roles from the start is exciting, because corporate America is so used to the "implement and fix" method, as opposed to the "do it right, do it once" mentality. Just knowing who is in your Corporate Family and how best to utilize their assets will increase your bottom line as you eliminate wasteful meetings and rework. Take the time in the beginning to identify who is in your Corporate Family and whether or not he or she is in the correct position, so that when you move forward, you will move with speed and efficiency.

CHAPTER FIVE

THE CONSTRUCTION

After you have set the context, and every member of your team has agreed to participate fully, it is time to walk them through the transformation process. I find it helpful to explain the multiple intelligences and Family Traits to them in the beginning. Whether you have them read this book ahead of time or whether you go through the traits with them is up to you. If you wish, you can obtain an electronic copy of the Family Traits from the previous chapter or a full workbook through my website (http://www.teamstofamilies.com) and use them during this process.

After your team understands the traits, have each person write down how much of each family member they embody. I had a Corporate Family member who I would say is 90 percent Mom and 10 percent Dad. I had another whom I would categorize as 30 percent Sister, 30 percent Cousin, and 40 percent Dad. Another was almost 100 percent Sister. Having them write down who they are helps them to clearly identify the traits and skills that they bring to the family. This will help in further discussions. There are some managers who like to have their employees identify the percentages of Family Traits that they see in their co-workers. Other managers stay away from that course. There is value in having an outside opinion state what he or she sees, and I have always enjoyed other people's impressions of me, as they give me valuable insight. Other people do not enjoy that type of input and find it upsetting and, at times, insulting. You know the makeup of your team's personalities. Take the course of action that is best for the cohesiveness of the team.

The next step is to have everyone write down the attributes that he or she associates with a positive family environment. Then have them list the negative attributes that sum up a dysfunctional family. Again, we are referring to the ideal family that each person has in his own mind that is created from his history and experience. Most of us know *Little House on the Prairie, The Waltons, The Andy Griffith Show* or other similar shows that embody some of these attributes. The purpose of this exercise is to get everyone to identify exactly what his or her Corporate Family will look like. The family must share and agree on desired positive attributes, so that everyone can work toward the same picture or vision and avoid wasting time trying to obtain different objectives. Below are some examples of positive and negative attributes.

Positive	Negative
1) Communication	1) Superstition
2) Nurturing	2) Rudeness
3) Loyalty	3) Selfishness
4) Sincerity	4) Sarcasm
5) Appreciation	5) Clique-oriented
6) Humor	6) Lying
7) Support	7) Favoritism
8) Fairness	8) Gossip
9) Honesty	9) Lack of respect

Family Values: Setting the House Rules

Once everyone has gone through these initial exercises and identified the type of family that they envision and expect to create, then you can begin addressing the individual issues surrounding your existing team by establishing Family Values. In order to create a solid Corporate Family, you need to go through the following three steps over and over until all of the issues have been addressed, and everyone is satisfied with the list of Family Values that has been created.

1) Identify an issue

2) Create a Family Value

3) Obtain everyone's affirmation

The first step is to identify an issue that is detrimental to the team. In other words, identify what is occurring on a frequent basis that is eroding the team's efficiency, chemistry, or communication. Is someone on the team leaving work undone at the end of the day? That issue could hurt the team's efficiency. Is someone failing to be respectful or cordial when passing on information? That issue could hurt the team's communication. Is someone talking about members of the team to other departments? That issue could hurt the team's chemistry. Any recurring issue that is centered around an action and not a mood or feeling should be identified as a target. Moods and feelings are impossible to regulate and legislate. Imagine if someone told you that you couldn't be frustrated at work. Your first reaction may actually be frustration at being told to not be frustrated. We will feel a myriad of emotions throughout the workday. Whether we allow those emotions to affect our work, our relationships, or our moods is up to us. A Family Value cannot be created to address whether or not a person can have those emotions. Instead, it is better to focus on a physical action or an event that is occurring and write that down. Here is an example:

> Any recurring issue that is centered around an action and not a mood or feeling should be identified as a target.

Issue:	Daily work is not completed by the end of the day.

After they have written down the issue, have them list the effects that the issue has on the team. Whether someone writes a bulleted list or a paragraph describing the ill effects, is each person's personal preference. The key is to identify the actual negative consequences of that action.

Issue:	Daily work is not completed by the end of the day.
Negative Effects:	Customer issues are not communicated to the other departments.
	There is a backlog first thing in the morning.
	Other team members end up doing the work.
	Daily reporting is incorrect.
	The whole team looks bad.

By listing the negative effects, it becomes clear to the entire team why this issue needs to be addressed. You may find that other members of the team will come up with additional negative effects. Write the issue and all the effects that are presented on the board or flip chart so that the issue is clear and in the open. This also acts as a psychological purging for the team members. Once something is written down, then the mind is able to let it go and move on. This catharsis is an essential part of this process. You also want to encourage your team to discuss verbally how this issue makes them feel. Make sure that everyone understands that these comments need to be focused on their experiences. Try to avoid comments like "When Joe doesn't finish his work, it ticks me off because I end up doing it all." A better statement would be "When work isn't finished at the end of the day, it causes more work in the morning." This revision isn't confrontational, and it avoids the "martyr mentality" by keeping the emphasis on how the problem affects the team. The "martyr mentality" comes into play when someone states as a point in fact that he is the only one affected or that he is the only one suffering. An issue affects the whole team, and nothing is gained by playing the victim. This can be a little tricky to explain (you may want to have your team read this chapter before beginning) and facilitate, but once everyone understands and runs through the first issue or two, then the rest of the issues will progress fairly smoothly.

Step two is to create a Family Value. I have also described this as a House Rule. A Family Value is a rule that the family unanimously agrees to implement for the benefit of the family as a whole. Again, this value should be addressing the issue and not the feeling or emotion behind it.

> A Family Value is a rule that the family unanimously agrees to implement for the benefit of the family as a whole.

CORPORATE FAMILIES

Issue:	Daily work is not completed by the end of the day.
Negative Effects:	Customer issues are not communicated to the other departments.
	There is a backlog first thing in the morning.
	Other team members end up doing the work.
	Daily reporting is incorrect.
	The whole team looks bad.
Family Value:	Complete all assigned work in the queue before clocking out.

As you can see, the Family Value is specific, clear, and short. You do not need a paragraph to communicate the value. It also speaks to the issue directly, and it is an action that can be accomplished. Sometimes, these Family Values come quickly and easily and seem extremely obvious (like this one). Other times, it seems like the Family Value goes through more revisions than the federal budget. If it appears that a proposed value is complex and the wording isn't covering everything, then try breaking it up into two separate Family Values. That can often help to solidify what is at the heart of the value and what is extraneous garbage.

THE CONSTRUCTION

It is important to note at this time that you are writing these values for the 80 percent of the time that this issue is occurring. The 80/20 rule can be applied here to say that every Family Value should address at least 80 percent or more of the issue. If our Family Value reads "Half the team needs to complete all their daily work before clocking out," then we can obviously see that it will not address 80 percent of the issue. (It is also not clear as to which half of the team it is referring to, not to mention that it is not uniform to the entire team.) Your team will always encounter events that happen outside the given processes of the company, and they must make adjustments to accomplish those tasks. The same is true with Family Values. You want to make sure that each Family Value covers the majority of the time that the issue occurs.

The example stated above seems fairly straightforward, but someone may ask about holidays or three-day weekends, or about people leaving early or taking half days off. Don't get bogged down in the anomalies. Trust that the family will pull together during those times to make sure that the work gets done by the close of day. If the team is not willing to trust in each other in that way, then write a Family Value that speaks to family members helping each other in times of crisis. Remember, this is their family—your family—and you must set your Family Values to reflect how you wish to work within your family.

Here are some more examples of Family Values to help spark some ideas of your own:

- ☐ What is said or done in the family stays in the family.

- ☐ Defend the family members by addressing the issue at hand and not who caused it.

- ☐ Assume the positive in any communication.

- ☐ Help without expectation of reciprocity.

- ☐ Follow through on promises and commitments.

The third and final step is the most important—to obtain everyone's affirmation. Everyone must agree on each Family Value. This cannot be a majority vote. It must be a unanimous vote. If even one person does not agree to the Family Value proposed, then it must either be discarded or changed until there is 100 percent agreement. The reason behind this stringent rule is that these are the Family Values that everyone must adhere to. There must be 100 percent buy-in from the entire family. If any individual is bullied or pressured into accepting a rule, then he or she will likely become a silent protestor who refuses to follow suit at the first opportunity. True unity takes a bit more time and effort. But the resulting cohesiveness is worth the time and pain of "working it out."

This process can take thirty minutes or eight hours, depending on who is in the family, how they currently inter-

> If even one person does not agree to the Family Value proposed, then it must either be discarded or changed until there is 100 percent agreement

act, what the issues are, and how invested they are in moving beyond the past and into the future. It can be fun and exciting or painful and stressful. Both choices, and all those in between, are good and productive. Remember, the point is to put this future family under pressure in a controlled environment (like the 1980 U.S. Olympic Hockey Team), so that when they are in their daily routine, they come together in support instead of attacking each other.

CHAPTER SIX

MAINTENANCE AND UPKEEP

HOW TO KEEP IT RUNNING

CONGRATULATIONS, YOU HAVE NOW ESTABLISHED your own Corporate Family. Sitting before you is a group of people who know who they are (Family Traits), know how they learn, process and communicate (multiple intelligences), and know how they want to work together (Family Values). Your Corporate Family is like a newborn baby. It may have been a painful, labor-intensive process getting it to this point, but it is here, and it is perfect. None of the Family Values have been broken. No family member has yet to be upset or irritated during the daily grind and, for the most part, everyone is happy.

When my first child was born, I held him in my arms and looked into his beautiful blue eyes and said, "You're perfect.

> When my first child was born, I held him in my arms and looked into his beautiful blue eyes and said, "You're perfect. I'll try my best not to screw you up too much."

I'll try my best not to screw you up too much." As a parent, you know you're going to make mistakes while raising your children. You're going to lose your temper, raise your voice, give them treats when they should not have them, discipline them too much for something and not enough for something else, and model the wrong behavior in front of them. You just have to know that you are going to make mistakes and hope and pray that the right choices you make dwarf all your errors.

Your Corporate Family is at that same point now. It is perfect, and no one in the family has done anything to screw it up yet ... but someone will. What do you do when a family member doesn't live up to the Family Values, and the entire Corporate Family is on the verge of collapsing? How do you keep your Corporate Family intact? The answer is simple but not easy:

Family members must hold each other accountable to the standards they have set.

If you recall *Little House on the Prairie*, then you probably remember scenes where Mary, the oldest child, would chide her sister Laura for her behavior. Mary had as much authority to correct Laura as did Ma and Pa. A family knows the rules and values and will correct a family member if he or she breaks the rules or behaves in a manner that is incongruent with the values they hold dear.

Your Corporate Family must also have the power to immediately call attention to any behavior that breaks a value. There are several reasons why the supervisor or manager cannot be the only one to play traffic cop. First, most managers are not around all day to see when a value is broken. Second, a manager's focus is typically on items that are higher up the company ladder. Third, and most important, a supervisor who has this traffic cop role could become a dictator or micromanager. In that scenario, many family members would probably begin to act like naughty little children, seeing how many values they could break without getting caught. There are always those who will push the limits of any boundary, especially if they believe that they are only accountable to one person. With a dictatorship, the new family would quickly collapse, due to the erosion of values and the lack of integrity. For this reason, it is the family members themselves who must police each other.

Sound daunting? It is. You won't find a typical corporate team meeting such a standard. Then again, you won't find a typical corporate team systematically decreasing turnover and burnout or increasing productivity and job satisfaction. The universal accountability inherent in a Corporate Family is

The universal accountability inherent in a Corporate Family is a paradigm shift for most companies and their employees.

a paradigm shift for most companies and their employees. But once you have universal accountability integrated into your team, you will be amazed at the transformation.

When a clear infraction has occurred, and the offender did not "catch" the mistake himself, another family member must hold him accountable. There are seven guidelines to successful accountability:

1) **Address the Family Value that was broken and not the family member who broke it.** This guideline is important for every family member to understand. It is based on a Biblical principle that roughly states "Hate the sin and not the sinner." The issue is not that the family member is a bad person or is intentionally trying to break the Family Values. The issue is that a value was broken, and the person needs to know that she broke it (she may be unaware that she did) because you know she broke it. Without accountability, that person may turn the breaking of values into a game, as stated above. Soon the entire family unit will fall apart. Families hold together because they don't let each other get away with breaking the rules. You, Corporate Family member, must not let your family members break the Family Values without saying something.

2) **Discuss the issue in private, not in public.** The discussion of the broken Family Value must be done in private. There is no reason for public humiliation. It is hard for someone to hear that he has made a mistake and broken a Family Value. Often times, it is even harder for the person who is pointing out the mistake. Performing the correction in public just makes it more difficult for both parties involved. Choose an appro-

priate time to discuss the broken value, and make sure that you are the only two people involved.

3) **State the Family Value that was broken.** Once you are in a private setting, you should start by stating the Family Value that was broken. That way both of you are on the same page as to what is being discussed. Then, explain in what way that Family Value was broken. Describe what the scenario or situation was that broke the value. For Example: "Mary, I would like to discuss the Family Value that states "Complete all assigned work in the queue before clocking out."

4) **Suggest an alternative course of action.** My mentor in college used to say that if you bring a problem to the table, then you had better bring a possible solution too. No one likes it when you bring up a problem or issue with the expectation that the group will solve it without your input. In other words, don't dump your problems on the group and then walk away. The same is true for your Corporate Family. If a Family Value has been broken, then you should suggest how that individual family member could have proceeded without breaking it. For example: "Rather than leave work undone until the next morning, perhaps one of us could have assisted you in completing the tasks. Would you be willing to ask us for help next time?"

5) **Thank the person for bringing up the broken value.** It is hard to approach someone and tell him that he

made a mistake, broke a value, and, essentially, let the whole family down. If you are the person who broke the value, then you need to thank the person who brought it to your attention, for his or her courage.

6) **Be open and accepting of what is being said, and know that it is true for that person.** It is hard to hear criticism and correction without getting defensive. We never like hearing how we messed up or were wrong, and we often defend our position without really hearing what the other person has to say.

William Shakespeare penned a wide variety of wretched and despicable characters. When I was studying his works, I learned an interesting fact: in all of the plays he wrote, Shakespeare created only one malicious character: Iago, from *Othello*. Every other character, no matter how evil he or she appeared to be, had noble intentions. These characters truly believed that what they were doing was in the best interests of whomever they represented, whether it was their country, other people, or themselves. People are not typically malicious in their intents and communications. For the most part, they speak and act according to what they see to be correct and just.

In the movie *Star Wars: Episode VI: Return of the Jedi*, Obi-Wan Kenobi says, "Luke, you are going to find that many of the truths we cling to depend greatly on our own point of view." This profound statement can serve to help us as we listen to criticism and correction. The person speaking is not trying to be cruel or malicious, and she isn't getting some sick satisfaction from calling you out. She is bringing up the issue from a place of truth and with the family's best interests at heart. Listen with that perspective in mind, and try not to rationalize your actions or defend yourself.

7) **If you broke a Family Value, then admit it and apologize.** There are many times when the only person who knows that you broke a value is you. This doesn't mean that it didn't happen. If *you* know it happened, then it happened. Be honest and truthful with yourself. If you can lie to yourself, then you can lie to anyone. Strive to hold yourself to a high standard, and work toward living a life of integrity. This intention doesn't have to be limited to your actions within your Corporate Family. I encourage you to live your life with integrity every day.

> If you can lie to yourself, then you can lie to anyone.

I remember a trip to the bank when I was about twelve years old. My mom went in and withdrew several hundred dollars in cash. When we got home, she counted the money in the envelope and realized that the teller had given her an extra one hundred dollar bill by mistake. What would you do in that instance? Would you keep the money or return it?

My mom called the bank, asked to speak with the teller, and explained the situation. The teller was so grateful, as she would have been in serious trouble for being one hundred dollars short when she cashed out her drawer at the end of the day. My mom drove back to the bank right away and returned the money. I'm sad to say that this example of living with integrity is getting more and more rare in today's society. Do you treat incorrect change as a gift, or do you correct the error? Strive to live your life with integrity. Be honest with yourself, and you'll be honest with those around you.

These guidelines for keeping the Family Values intact are essential to follow. Without them, family members soon dismiss the values and quickly forget them. Before long, you will be back to the dysfunction you are currently experiencing.

The other key to holding the family unit together is the establishment of Family Traditions (as I described in chapter 2). These traditions usually come from within the family and need to be supported and strengthened by everyone, including management. (Three O'Clock Chocolate was very popular with my Corporate Family.) See my website (www.teamstofamilies.com) for more examples of Family Traditions.

FINAL THOUGHTS

Your Corporate Family now has all the basic components it needs to survive and thrive. But you should remember that it takes energy and input to grow a relationship. Without the support of everyone in the family and management, it will be almost impossible to succeed in transforming your team. There will be many obstacles in your path.

The first obstacle is any history or "bad blood" that may exist between the family members. There may be bridges that are damaged, scorched, or completely destroyed. These family members must be willing to forgive, forget, and rebuild those bridges.

Another big obstacle is pre-programming. Throughout our lives, we have been taught to do things a certain way. In school, we were taught that talking or helping during class was cheating, and we were disciplined for it. In business, cross-functional teams and collaboration are encouraged, in order to solve problems. Some people have the belief that their fellow team members are merely rungs to be stepped on as they climb up the corporate ladder. These people don't have the Corporate Family mindset and will need to be ready, willing, and able to transform. There are countless articles that state that people in the workforce genuinely desire to do a good job. Most people are interested in working toward something bigger than themselves and producing high quality work that is highly regarded. Refer back to the statement in the former chapter (Guideline #6): People are not typically malicious in their intents and communications. Every person wants to do good work and improve, but some may need to change pre-programming to achieve better results. Everyone wants his team to be the best team, and everyone will want his Corporate Family to succeed and be a model for the rest of the organization.

> People are not typically malicious in their intents and communications.

Can you imagine what would happen if your Corporate Family became the template for all the other divisions in the company? How many other departments can you name that are in need of team improvements or complete team overhauls? How much easier would your job be if the information and cooperation you were getting from other teams improved? How effective would the company be if it employed only Corporate Family units? In his book, *The Five Dysfunctions of a Team: A Leadership Fable*, Patrick Lencioni states, "If you could get all of the people in an organization rowing in the same direction, you could dominate any industry in any market against any competition at any time." Establish Corporate Families throughout your company, and watch how far and fast it grows.

Now that you have learned the basics of the Corporate Family system, you are prepared to begin creating your own Corporate Family. However, as I have pointed out several times, this type of change is not easy for many people. It is best to treat this as a process, and plan to reinforce the concepts and policies periodically. If you want or need additional support in implementing your Corporate Family, there are several options available to you. I have found that hearing this information presented in a seminar format from an outside source can be transformational for managers and teams with a significant entrenched history. In fact, having an entire team attend a seminar is the best way to achieve unity and buy-in, because it allows team members to distance themselves from day-to-day issues and focus on transformation. If you choose to lead this transformation alone, there are presentation materials and workbooks available as well. For more information regarding upcoming seminars, private consultations, and additional supporting materials, please visit www.teamstofamilies.com.

Printed in the USA
CPSIA information can be obtained
at www.ICGtesting.com
JSHW082222140824
68134JS00015B/678